Addison Wesley
Science & Technology 5

Energy and Control
•
Conservation of Energy

Steve Campbell   Jim Wiese

Douglas Hayhoe   Beverley Williams

Doug Herridge   Ricki Wortzman

Lionel Sandner

PEARSON

Addison
Wesley

Toronto

Coordinating & Developmental Editors
Jenny Armstrong
Lee Geller
Lynne Gulliver
John Yip-Chuck

Editors
Susan Berg
Jackie Dulson
Christy Hayhoe
Sarah Mawson
Mary Reeve
Keltie Thomas

Researchers
Paulee Kestin
Louise MacKenzie
Karen Taylor
Wendy Yano, Colborne Communications Centre

Consultants
Dr. Ron Kydd, Professor and Head of Chemistry, University of Calgary
Lynn Lemieux, Sir Alexander MacKenzie Sr. P.S., Toronto District School Board

Pearson Education Canada would like to thank the teachers and consultants who reviewed and field-tested this material.

Design
Pronk&Associates

ISBN 0–201–64987–X

This book contains recycled product and is acid free.
Printed and bound in Canada.

7 8 – TCP – 08 07

Conservation of Energy

The physical universe is made up of only two things—matter and energy. Each plays a big part in our lives. In this unit, you're going to investigate energy. You'll find it everywhere—even in places you might not think of! Energy is in everything you do in your life. Energy from the sun heats Earth and lets plants make food. The energy in food lets you run, play, and learn in school. Energy is used to power everything from the lights in your home, to the family car. Will this energy last forever? What does using energy cost us?

Now you will find out:

- what energy does and how energy can be changed from one form to another

- ways to use renewable and non-renewable energy sources wisely in order to conserve energy

- how to design and make machines that transform energy to do a specific task

- how our use of energy affects our environment

Energy Hunt

Get Started

Energy makes things go. Energy does work. Energy turns lights on and heats your home. Energy makes your body work and your brain think. Energy makes the world go round. Think about the many ways that you use energy every day. You use energy to make your breakfast and to get to school. You use it in the batteries that power your video games, in the lights that let you read this book, and even in the food you eat. What other ways do you use energy?

Work On It

Let's go on an energy hunt to find the energy in our lives.

1. Copy this chart on a separate sheet of paper.

2. In a small group, look at the picture above and start filling in the chart.

Energy device	Use of energy	Where the energy comes from
Lights	Let us see	Electricity
Car	Helps us move	Fuel

Communicate

Write   Discuss

1. Compare your chart with those done by other groups. What other uses of energy are there that your group did not find? Add these to your chart.

2. Look at the many ways that energy is used. Which use of energy is the most common? Why do you think this is the most common use of energy compared with other forms?

Build On What You Know   HOME

Tonight, start a separate chart, similar to the one you started today, but add 3 more empty columns to the right side of your chart. Use this new chart to record the ways that you use energy in your home. What ways are similar to the energy uses in this picture? What ways are different? Keep your chart handy in an Energy File. This can be a file folder or large envelope.

1 Energy Everywhere

Get Started

In your energy hunt, you discovered that energy is everywhere. It's in the food you eat, in the electricity that powers your lights, and even in the games you play. Let's look further at what energy can do.

Work On It

In this activity, you will investigate energy by experimenting with different devices that use energy. Your teacher will set up four energy exploration centres where you will test the devices. As you perform this activity, think about how you would define energy.

Make a table like the one shown here to organize the information you will collect at each centre. One device is included in the table as an example.

Device	Observations	Energy involved
Wind-up toy car	After I wind up the car and place it on the floor, it moves	Energy I use when I wind it up Energy the toy car uses when it moves

Centre 1

Materials for each group:

safety goggles

rubber band

10 cm piece of a strong plastic straw

wind-up toy car

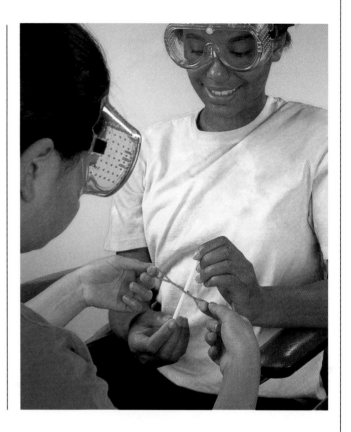

Procedure

1 Put on the safety goggles. Place the rubber band over the two index fingers of one member of your group. Insert the straw in the middle of the rubber band, and rotate the straw so it twists the rubber band. Rotate the straw 10 times and then release it. What happens?

2 Wind up the toy car and place it on the floor. What happens?

Centre 2

Materials for each group:

two bar magnets

iron nails

iron filings

paper clips

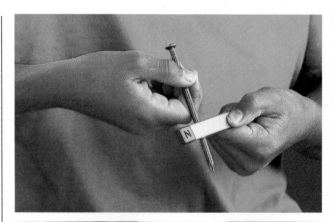

Procedure

1 Bring one magnet near the iron nails, iron filings, and paper clips.

2 Bring the N-pole of one magnet toward the S-pole of the other magnet. What happens? Turn one of the magnets around and bring two like poles together. What happens?

Centre 3

Materials for each group:
electric timer   lamp   hair dryer

Procedure

1 Plug the lamp into the electric timer. Set the timer to activate in 5 min. What happens?

2 Turn on the hair dryer. What happens?

Centre 4

Materials for each group:
guitar or other stringed instrument
solar calculator reading lamp

Procedure

1 Pluck one string of the guitar. What happens?

2 Turn on the lamp and shine it on the solar cell of the calculator. Use the calculator to multiply 152 by 7659. What happens? Describe what happens when you cover and uncover the solar cell.

Communicate  Write Discuss Present

1. List the different ways energy is being used in the devices you tested.

2. Did any of the devices store energy for later use? If so, describe how energy was stored and released later.

3. Was the use of energy controlled in any of the devices you investigated? If so, explain how it was controlled.

4. Discuss with your group what a good definition of energy would be. Present your definition to your classmates. Explain why you decided on this definition.

If Time Allows

1. Write down any questions you have about the devices you used at the different centres.

2. Choose one question about one device that you would like to investigate. Plan an investigation for your question using the headings below.

Problem: What do you want to find out?

Materials: What equipment would you need to do your investigation?

Procedure: What steps would you take to complete your investigation?

Observations: What results would you collect or measure, and how would you show them?

2 Forms of Energy

Get Started
· ·

At the beginning of this unit, you went on an energy hunt. You looked at some of the many ways that you use energy. You probably noticed that you don't always use the same kind of energy. When you cook dinner on the stove, you use heat. And when you turn on a lamp, you use electricity. But when you read next to a lamp, you use light. Grouping energy uses together shows you examples of different kinds of energy. Heat is one. Electricity and light are others. These different kinds of energy are called forms of energy.

Scientists define **energy** as the ability to make things move and do work. All energy can be classified as either **potential energy** or **kinetic energy.** Think of potential energy as stored energy that can be used to make things move and do work. Kinetic energy is the energy in any moving object. Energy is also commonly classified into many different forms. As you read about these different forms, think about other examples of where you might see or use these forms of energy.

Sound energy is the energy produced when matter vibrates. When sound energy enters our ears, it makes parts of our ears move. These moving parts send signals to our brain, telling us what we are hearing.

Heat or **thermal energy** is in every object. If an object has a lot of thermal energy, it feels hot. If an object has very little thermal energy, it feels cold. We use thermal energy to cook and to keep our homes warm. A steam engine on an old train uses thermal energy to make the train move.

Light energy is a form of energy that allows us to see things. When light energy enters our eyes, it causes special signals to move from our eyes to our brains. These signals tell us what we are looking at.

Mechanical energy is the energy due to the position of an object or the movement of an object. Mechanical energy can be in the form of potential energy or kinetic energy. A moving bicycle has mechanical energy in the form of kinetic energy.

Chemical energy is the stored energy in substances that can be released in chemical reactions. The chemical energy in gasoline is used to make a car move. Our bodies use chemical energy in food to help us move and do things.

Electrical energy is the energy we use to activate parts in our machines, such as in televisions and computers. We also use it to operate lights and some heating systems.

Gravitational energy is the stored energy an object has because of its position above Earth's surface. A ball held up in the air has gravitational energy. If you let it go, it moves down toward Earth.

Elastic energy is the stored energy an object has when its shape is changed by stretching (pulling apart) or compressing (pushing together). A stretched rubber band and a compressed spring have elastic energy stored in them. When you let go of the rubber band or the spring, they will move.

Nuclear energy is the energy stored deep inside matter. Special kinds of technology are needed to release nuclear energy in radioactive substances, such as uranium. When nuclear energy is released, it can be used to make electricity.

Magnetic energy is the energy stored in some magnet systems. When you bring the like poles of two magnets together, they move apart. If you bring the unlike poles of two magnets close to each other, they move closer together.

Communicate Write

1. In the activities in lesson one, you observed energy being used in different devices. Make a chart which lists the devices you investigated in one column. In a column next to each device, write the forms of energy that were involved when you used it.

2. Give an example for each of the following forms of energy from your own life. For example, you use light energy and electrical energy when you watch television.

   a. thermal energy (heat)

   b. chemical energy

   c. sound energy

   d. elastic energy

3. a. What definition do scientists use for energy?

   b. At the end of the last section, you presented your own definition of energy. In what way was it similar to the scientific definition? In what way was it different?

Build On What You Know

Look again at your chart of energy uses in your Energy File. Look at the groups of energy uses that you identified. Are your groups similar or different to the form of energy described in this section? Write the scientific name of the form of energy (e.g., sound energy) in the column next to your similar energy groups.

Get Started

Most of the time when you use energy, you are using more than one form
of energy. You start with one form, and it turns into another one. When you
switch on a lamp, you use electrical energy, which becomes light energy.
This change of energy from one form to another is called an **energy
transformation**. For the lamp to work, electrical energy is transformed
into light energy. In a car, the chemical energy in gasoline is transformed
into kinetic energy, as the car moves. Sometimes, an energy transformation
can result in more than one form of energy. When a candle burns, the
chemical energy of candle wax is transformed into heat and light. Can
you think of other examples of energy transformations?

Suppose you could measure the amount of energy at the beginning and end of an energy transformation. You would always find that you end up with the same amount of energy that you started with. The energy would be in different forms, but the total amount would be the same. Scientists have been able to measure many energy transformations. They have found that energy never disappears. They also found that no new energy is ever created. Another way of saying this is that energy cannot be created or destroyed. It can only be transformed from one form to another.

Transformations make energy very useful to us. We can store energy in one form until we need it. Then, we can transform it into other forms that we can use. When you take your lunch to school, you are taking the chemical energy stored in your food. Later, when you eat the food, your body will transform it into forms of energy you need—kinetic energy for movement and thermal energy to keep you warm.

In this activity, you will investigate energy transformation and storage in two devices which you will make. Be sure to record your observations as you work.

Wind-Up Tractor

Materials for each pair:

thread spool	thumb tack
plastic washer	button
wooden ramp	

rubber band about the same length as the spool

strong wooden toothpick

candle slice with a hole in the middle

Procedure

1 Slip the rubber band through the hole in the thread spool. You want it to pass from one end of the spool through to the other.

2 Attach one end of the rubber band to the spool with the thumb tack.

3 Slip the other end of the rubber band through the hole in the washer.

4 Put a wooden toothpick through the loop in the rubber band that sticks out through the hole in the washer.

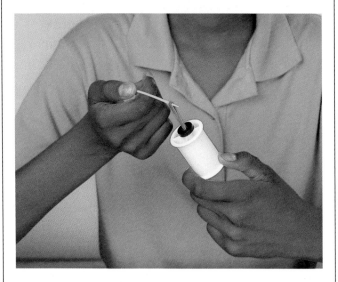

5 Turn the toothpick to wind up the rubber band inside the spool. Remember how many times you wound it up. You have just built a wind-up tractor.

6 Place the tractor on a table or floor and let it go. What happens?

7 Try winding the rubber band a different number of times. Measure the distance the tractor travels each time. What do you notice?

8 Try having your wind-up tractor travel up a ramp. Predict how the distance it travels uphill will compare with the distance it travels on level ground. Test your prediction.

9 Try different-sized spools and rubber bands for your tractor. Do they make the tractor go faster or farther? Try other materials instead of the plastic washer. Will a button or a candle slice with a hole in the middle work?

Come-Back Can

Materials for each pair:

two nails	8 cm of string
hammer	tape
coffee can with plastic lid	
rubber band slightly longer than the height of the coffee can	
several weights (heavy nuts and bolts)	

Procedure

1 Use the hammer and a nail to punch a hole in the centre of the plastic lid and the bottom of the coffee can.

2 Attach weights to the rubber band as shown. One good way to do this is to tie the string tightly around both the weights and the rubber band.

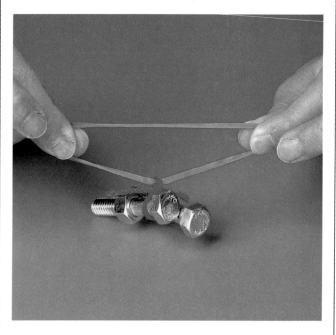

3 Slip the rubber band through the hole in the bottom of the can from inside. Put a nail through the loop in the rubber band. Tape the nail to the can securely.

4 Pull the remaining end of the rubber band through the hole in the plastic lid. Put a nail through the loop in the rubber band. Tape the nail to the lid securely. Snap the lid onto the can.

5 Gently roll the can away from you on a hard, smooth, flat surface. What happens?

Communicate
Write

1. Answer these questions for the wind-up tractor and then for the come-back can. Organize your answers into a chart.

   a. What makes the device move?

   b. Where is the energy coming from?

   c. What energy transformation is involved in each device? What form of energy did you start with? What form of energy did you end with?

   d. How is energy stored in each device?

2. How are the energy transformations similar in both devices? How are they different?

3. For the wind-up tractor, do you think there is more energy, less energy, or the same amount of energy at the end of the transformation?

4. What happens when you wind up the rubber band of your tractor many more times? If you wind it up twice as many times, does it travel twice as far?

5. Some wind-up tractors move faster or go farther than others. Why do you think this happens? How could you test your ideas?

6. Give an example of a device in which each of the following energy transformations occurs. For example, in a hair dryer, electrical energy is transformed to thermal energy.

   a. electrical energy $\xrightarrow{\text{to}}$ sound energy

   b. chemical energy $\xrightarrow{\text{to}}$ thermal energy

   c. elastic energy $\xrightarrow{\text{to}}$ kinetic energy

   d. chemical energy $\xrightarrow{\text{to}}$ thermal energy

   e. gravitational energy $\xrightarrow{\text{to}}$ kinetic energy

7. Complete the following statement: Energy cannot be created or destroyed but can only _____ .

Build On What You Know

Return to your home energy chart in your Energy File. What are the main ways that you and your family use energy in your home? What energy transformations are involved in those energy uses? List those energy transformations in a new column on your chart. What are the main forms of energy that these energy transformations start with? Why do you think these energy forms are used so much?

4 Moving Along

Get Started

In the last activity, you built devices that moved because they
transformed elastic energy into kinetic energy. Other energy
transformations can end with kinetic energy as well. Your challenge
is to design and build a device that uses an energy transformation
to cause it to move at least 2 m.

Think about the energy transformations you have investigated. What energy transformations could end with a moving object? What form of energy will you start with? How will you transform it into kinetic energy?

Materials for each group:

paper

pencils

pencil crayons or felt-tip pens

any materials in the classroom or at home, including those from the other activities you've done

Procedure

1 In your group, brainstorm ideas for a device you could build that uses an energy transformation to make it move. Make a list of your ideas. Choose the best one from your list.

2 Make a plan to turn your design idea into a self-powered device that can move 2 m. Think about how to make the energy transformation provide enough energy to move your device the entire distance. Sketch your device so you can see clearly how it will work.

3 Decide on the materials you will need. Collect them. If you can't get the materials you want for your design, you may have to redesign your device. What changes will you have to make?

4 Build your device. Test it and make any changes needed to help it work.

1. a. What energy transformations did you use in your device?

   b. How well did your device do what you thought it would?

   c. How would you change your device to improve its performance?

2. a. What did you learn about designing devices in this activity?

   b. How well did your team work together? Explain your answer.

3. Demonstrate your device to your classmates. Make sure that you list and explain the energy transformations involved in your device.

5 Energy Sources

By now, you know that you use energy in many different forms every day—electrical, sound, heat, light, and others. These forms of energy are transformed from other sources so that you can use energy for your needs. Where do the energy forms you use come from?

When you turn on a radio, you get sound energy. You know that it was transformed from electrical energy. But where did the electrical energy come from? It came from an electricity generating station that transforms other forms of energy into electrical energy. It might be a **hydro-electric power plant**, which uses flowing water to produce electricity. Or it might be a **nuclear generating station**, which uses the nuclear energy in a substance called uranium to produce electricity. Or it might be a generating station that uses oil or natural gas to produce electricity. Oil, natural gas, uranium, and water are examples of sources of energy. A **source of energy** is a material that is used to produce energy.

Before light bulbs and electric furnaces were invented, people burned oil from animal fat for light, and wood for heat.

Work On It

Read this information about energy sources with your partner. You might already know some of it, but you may also learn something new. Before you start to read, place a piece of paper between you and your partner. Write the words "energy sources" in the centre of the paper and circle it. As you read, add more information to create a mind map about energy sources.

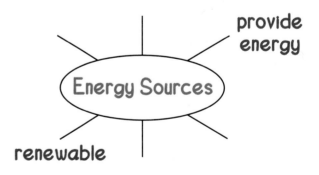

provide energy

Energy Sources

renewable

Our world depends on energy. At the beginning of this unit, you looked at some of the ways energy is used at school, in your community, and at home. Although you use many different forms of energy every day, that energy comes from only a few sources.

Hundreds of years ago, people depended more on the energy of their own bodies and that of animals to carry things and travel from place to place. They used wood for cooking and heating. Candles made from animal fat gave them light. People relied mainly on renewable energy sources.

A **renewable energy source** is one that is being replaced all the time. The sun, plants, wind, and water are examples of renewable energy sources. Wood can be considered to be a renewable energy source if we plant enough trees to replace the ones we use.

Today we rely mainly on non-renewable energy sources. A **non-renewable energy source** is an energy source that cannot be replaced once it is used up. New supplies are not being created or take too long to produce. Coal, oil, natural gas, and uranium are examples of non-renewable energy sources. They are formed over millions of years, inside Earth, but our current supplies of these energy sources will run out in less than a hundred years.

> **All renewable and non-renewable energy sources are part of our natural resources. Any material from nature that can be used by humans is a natural resource.**

About 250 years ago, people started using more non-renewable energy sources. Machines were being invented that required lots of energy. Many forests had been cut down for wood, so people had to find other energy sources. People needed energy sources that could be transported easily to where they were needed. They also needed energy sources that could be stored easily, so they could get the energy when they needed it.

Non-renewable energy sources like coal and oil were easier to transport and store than renewable energy sources like wind, sunshine, and animal fat. Also, energy sources like coal and oil could be used in the engines of the new machinery.

The first trains got their energy by burning coal.

Today we are surrounded by machinery and equipment that need energy to keep operating. We rely on cars, buses, and airplanes to get us to where we want to go. Furnaces keep us warm during the cold Canadian winter. Lights make it easier for us to read, work around the house, and play games at any time of day or night. Machines and other devices have made our lives much easier. But by using them, we are using up more of Earth's natural resources and affecting the environment. With non-renewable sources such as coal, oil, and natural gas, the more we use now, the less there will be in the future. Unfortunately, it's still too expensive to use renewable sources like solar energy to supply the energy needed to operate vehicles and many other devices.

Most vehicles on the roads today get their energy from burning gasoline or diesel fuel, which are made from oil.

This car uses the sun's energy as fuel. But you won't be seeing solar cells like these on your family car any time soon. This technology is very expensive.

1. What is the difference between a renewable energy source and a non-renewable energy source? Give two examples of each.

2. One of the ways our society has changed has been through the increasing use of machines and other technology.
   a. How have new devices made our lives easier and more enjoyable?
   b. How have these devices changed our use of energy?

3. Ask an adult at home to name two energy-using devices that you have now that they didn't have when they were younger. How would your life be different if you didn't have these devices?

4. Complete your mind map, if you haven't already done so. With your partner, use the information from your mind map to write an eight-line poem about energy sources. Your partner writes the first line, then you write the second line. Keep alternating lines until you finish the poem. Read your poem to your class.

Build On What You Know

Look again at your energy chart in your Energy File. What are the sources for the energy that you use? List them in a new column on your chart. Which of these energy sources are renewable and which are non-renewable? Write an "R" for renewable or an "NR" for non-renewable next to each energy source on your chart.

6 Non-renewable Energy Sources

If you travel across western Canada or southwestern Ontario, you'll see oil well pumps like this one scattered over the land. These pumps move slowly up and down to bring fossil fuel out of the ground, 24 h a day.

Get Started

Non-renewable energy sources include coal, oil, natural gas, and uranium. Coal, oil, and natural gas are called fossil fuels. A fuel is any material that releases energy when it is used. **Fossil fuels** were formed over millions of years from dead plants and animals. This dead matter was slowly covered by soil and rock. More soil and rock collected, burying it deeper and deeper. The pressure and heat from being buried deep in Earth changed the dead matter to coal, oil, or natural gas. These energy sources can be removed from Earth only by mining or drilling and pumping. Once they have been removed and used, no new coal, oil, or natural gas is available. Have you ever visited a coal mine or seen an oil or natural gas well? Describe the mine or well to your classmates.

Start a list of the advantages and disadvantages of each energy source that you read about. Add to your list as you study each energy source in this unit. You may want to use a table like this one.

Energy source	Advantages	Disadvantages
Coal		
Oil		

Coal

Coal, which is the most plentiful fossil fuel, has been used for heating for thousands of years. About 250 years ago, coal became an important energy source for many other uses. At that time, the steam engine and other machinery were invented. This machinery needed an energy source that was easy to transport and store and could produce a lot of energy. Coal was soon used to heat homes, fuel trains and ships, and power the machinery in factories. Today, it is used mainly to produce electricity. Over half of the world's electricity is produced by burning coal.

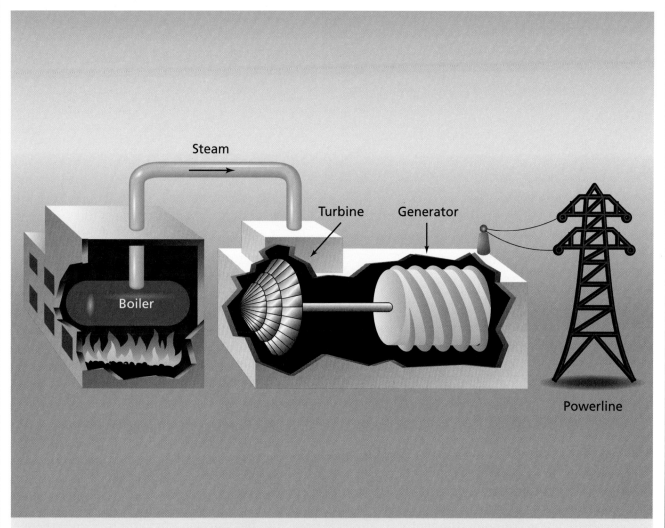

In this power plant, coal is burned to heat water into steam. The steam then moves very quickly past huge **turbines**, which are special wheels that spin very fast. The turbines are connected to a generator which produces electricity.

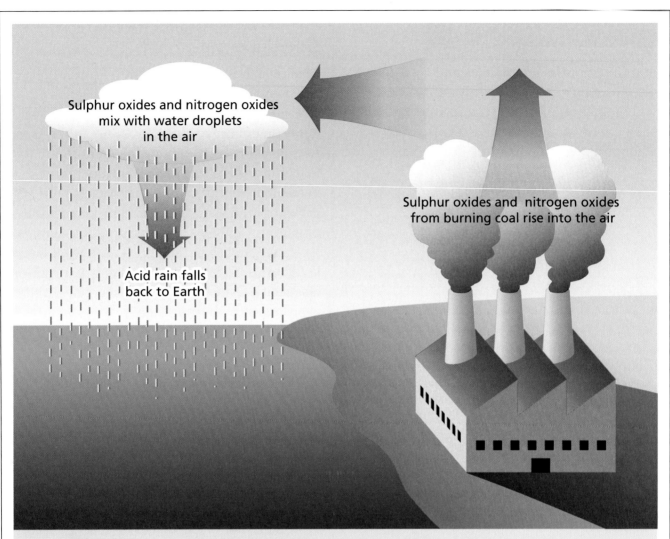

Sulphur oxides and nitrogen oxides mix with water droplets in the air

Acid rain falls back to Earth

Sulphur oxides and nitrogen oxides from burning coal rise into the air

One problem with burning coal is that it causes acid rain, which damages water, soil, and plants.

Coal is mined either underground or at Earth's surface, by first removing plants and soil. Mining is dirty and dangerous work. Surface mines damage the environment, although mining companies try to limit the damage.

Burning coal is a major cause of **acid rain**. As coal burns, it produces many gases, including sulphur oxides and nitrogen oxides. These gases combine with water droplets in the air to form acids. When these water droplets containing acids form rain and fall to the ground, we call it **acid rain**. If the air temperature is cold enough, the water droplets will fall as **acid snow**. Acid rain and snow are sometimes referred to as acid precipitation, and both cause damage to lakes, soil, and plants. Scientists and engineers are working on new technologies for power plants to cut down the amount of sulphur oxides and nitrogen oxides that coal puts into the air, to reduce acid precipitation.

Oil

Oil is pumped out of wells from deep underground. Before it can be used, it must be processed. This processing takes out unwanted chemicals and breaks the oil into different products. These products include gasoline, heating oil, airplane fuel, and diesel fuel. Raw materials to make plastics also come from oil. The oil from a well goes to a refinery for processing. It gets there by pipelines and oil tankers. After the refining process, the useful products from the oil are transported again. They are taken by pipelines, trains, trucks, and tankers to where people need them.

Huge supertankers like this one can carry more than 450 000 t of oil to refineries.

While oil provides us with energy and other useful products, it can be harmful to the environment. Sometimes accidents happen when oil is being transported. A pipeline might leak, poisoning the ground and water. An oil tanker might run into rocks and break up, spilling oil which affects marine life.

Natural Gas

Like oil, natural gas is pumped out of deep wells. It is an odourless gas that is used mainly for heating and as a fuel for some vehicles. Natural gas does not pollute the air when it burns, the way oil and coal do. However, some natural gas contains a poisonous chemical called hydrogen sulfide. This must be removed before the natural gas can be used. Like coal and oil, there is only a limited supply of natural gas.

Here are the locations of the major generating stations across Canada that use fossil fuels.

Uranium

Electricity from nuclear energy is produced from energy stored deep within a metal called uranium. Canadian scientists and engineers have developed one type of nuclear power plant called the Canadian Deuterium Uranium reactor, or CANDU reactor. The CANDU reactor releases the energy in uranium to heat water into steam. The steam is then used to spin turbines connected to generators, to create electricity. On average, about 25% of Canada's electricity is produced from nuclear energy. Some provinces, like Ontario, get over 40% of their electricity from nuclear energy.

No burning is needed to produce electricity this way, so using nuclear energy to produce electricity is cleaner than burning fossil fuels. Also, nuclear energy doesn't require a large amount of fuel. A lot of energy can be released from a small amount of uranium. In fact, one CANDU nuclear reactor can produce electricity for a year from a quantity of fuel about the size of a two-car garage. It would take 10 million tonnes of coal to produce the same amount of energy. That amount of coal would fill a train stretching from Toronto to Thunder Bay, Ontario. Currently, there is enough uranium to keep all the nuclear reactors in Canada running for the next 100 years.

But nuclear power has its problems too. The uranium used in nuclear power plants is dangerous to living things. It remains dangerous for thousands of years after it is used. With nuclear power, people worry about two things. What if there were an accident at the power station and some of the dangerous material leaked out? How can the waste material be kept safely for thousands of years, so it doesn't affect people and the environment? Despite these concerns, using nuclear energy to produce electricity has been relatively safe and clean for over 35 years.

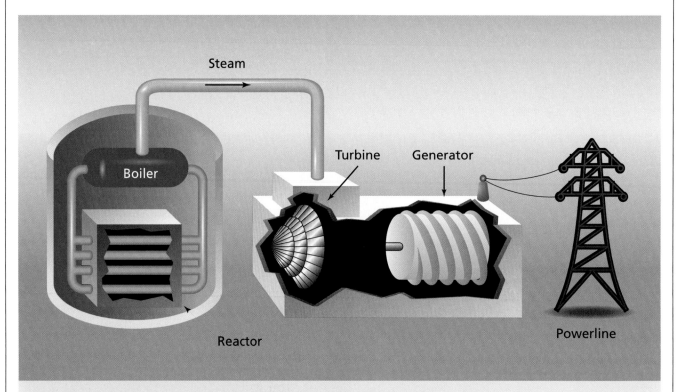

At nuclear power stations, uranium is used instead of fossil fuels to heat water into steam.
The steam then turns the turbines connected to a generator to make electricity.

Making an Oil Boom

Sometimes, large oil tankers have accidents that are very harmful to the environment. Huge waves caused by bad weather can sometimes cause a tanker to run into rocks under water and break up. An oil tanker can spill thousands of litres of oil into an ocean. The oil then kills fish, seabirds, and other marine animals, and pollutes shorelines.

If a tanker has spilled a lot of oil into a large body of water, clean-up crews will often use oil booms to contain the spill. An **oil boom** is a floating device that looks like a string of floats used to separate the deep end of a swimming pool from the shallow end. Oil booms, however, are much bigger and longer.

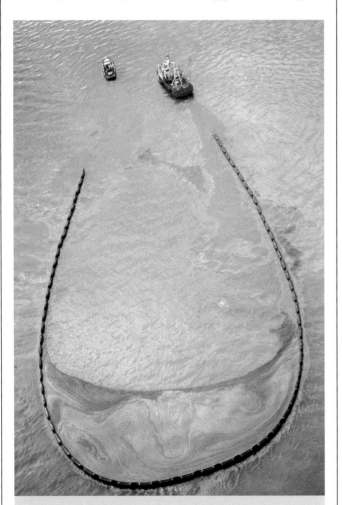

Can you see the oil boom in this picture? Do you think it's doing a good job of containing this oil spill?

Clean-up crews will use oil booms to surround the oil spill and stop it from spreading. Then they use huge vacuums to suck up the oil from the surface of the water and put it into another ship.

In this activity, your group will experiment with different materials to make an oil boom.

Materials for each group:

large plastic tub	Popsicle sticks
cooking oil	masking tape
blue food colouring	
large plastic straws	
500 mL measuring cup	
wooden barbecue skewers	
strips of paper or rags about 2 cm wide by 10 cm long	
any other materials you might think of	

Procedure

1. Fill the tub with water. This will be your ocean, and the sides of the tub will be your shorelines.

2. Add some food colouring to the water so you can see the oil better when you spill the oil on top of the water.

3. Now you are ready to try different designs for your oil boom. Choose the materials that you think will work best. Remember, your boom is supposed to contain the oil spill in a small area and prevent it from reaching the shoreline (the edge of the tub).

4. Repeat your experiment a few times using different designs for your boom and different sizes of oil spills. Since you will be doing your experiment a few times, you should think about the **variables** you need to control.

All the things that could affect what happens in an experiment are called variables. In any experiment, a scientist wants to test only one thing. But there might be many things that could change the results of an experiment. If you want to test only one of them, you have to keep the other ones the same.

5 As you test your boom designs, record your observations. You may want to use charts or tables to organize your results, and to keep track of all the variables.

6 Test a few different boom designs until you have decided on the best designs for certain sizes of oil spills.

Communicate

Discuss

Have a class discussion about the following topics.

1. Burning fossil fuels pollutes the environment. Why do we keep using these fuels? What can we do about the way they affect the environment?

2. a. How have people in Canada benefited from nuclear energy?

b. Should we continue to use nuclear energy?

3. Transporting oil over long distances can damage the environment. What could be done to prevent or reduce this damage?

4. How do you think oil spills affect fish, seabirds, and other marine animals?

If Time Allows

Use the Internet or old newspaper clippings at the library to research recent accidents involving oil tankers or pipelines. Have any recent accidents happened in, or close to Canada? Write 3 or 4 paragraphs about a recent oil spill and discuss it with your class. Remember to include in your report how the oil spill was cleaned up. Also, mention any new techniques being developed to deal with spills.

7 Water Power

Get Started

For over 2000 years, moving water has been used to turn water wheels in mills. A mill would be built next to a river or stream. The water would flow over or under the wheel and make it turn. The water wheel was connected to gears that turned a large round stone inside the mill. This stone was used to grind grain into flour. In Canada, only a few old mills operate now, mainly as museums.

Water is still an important energy source in Canada, but now it is used to produce electricity. Electricity produced in this way is called **hydro-electricity** (hydro means water). Almost 60% of the electricity in Canada comes from **hydro-electric power plants**.

Most hydro-electric power plants include two main parts: a dam and a generating station. A dam across a river holds water above the level of a generating station downstream. The generating station houses a set of turbines connected to a generator. The dammed water has gravitational potential energy because it is above the generating station. Water is allowed to flow down from behind the dam and through the turbines in the generating station. As the water flows down, its gravitational potential energy is transformed into kinetic energy. As the water passes through the turbines, some of its kinetic energy is transferred to the turbines, causing them to spin. The spinning turbines produce an electric current in the generator, transforming the kinetic energy of the turbines into electrical energy. Power lines connected to the generating station carry the electrical energy to where it is needed.

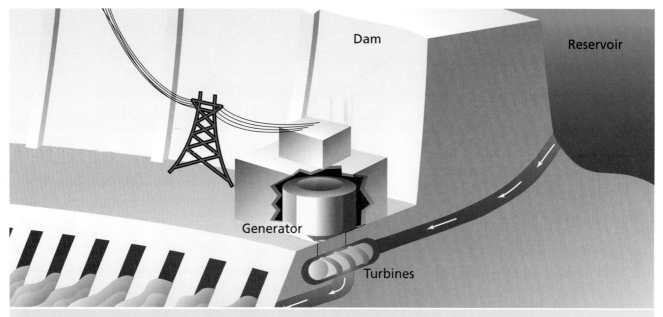

The gravitational potential energy of the water behind the dam is transformed into kinetic energy as the water flows down through the dam and spins the turbines. The generator transforms the kinetic energy of the spinning turbines into electrical energy.

Some hydro-electric power plants are built next to natural waterfalls, like this one at Niagara Falls.

Hydro-electric power is very clean energy. Nothing has to be burned to produce it, so no pollutants escape into the air. However, hydro-electric power plants are expensive to build. Huge dams must be built to create the large human-made lake behind the dam. This lake is called a **reservoir**. Reservoirs are created by flooding large areas of land. Often, people and animals who live in the area have to move to make way for the dam and reservoir.

In the next activity, you will investigate how water can turn a wheel. In the real world, this could be a water wheel for a mill or it could be a turbine in a huge hydro-electric generating station.

4 Test to see if your water wheel can spin freely by turning it with your hand.

Materials for each pair:

sink or large pan	masking tape
cup	water
plastic film canister with holes in top and bottom	
plastic margarine container with holes on opposite sides	
wooden barbecue skewer	
cardboard or construction paper	

Procedure

1 If your teacher has not already done so, make one hole at the top and one at the bottom of the film canister. Make holes on opposite sides of the margarine container, near the top. The holes in the margarine container must be big enough to let the skewer spin freely.

2 Use the masking tape and cardboard to create four or five flaps on the sides of the film canister, as shown in the photo.

3 Stick the skewer through the hole on one side of the margarine container, then through the film canister, and finally through the hole on the opposite side of the margarine container.

5 Place the margarine container and the water wheel in the sink or large pan. Use the cup to pour water onto the flaps of your water wheel. What happens?

6 What do you think would happen if you poured water onto the wheel from different heights? Test your prediction.

7 What do you think would happen if you changed the number, shape, or size of the flaps on your water wheel? How would any of these changes affect the way your water wheel works? Make predictions and test your ideas.

Here are the locations of the major generating stations across Canada that use moving water as the energy source.

Communicate  Write   Discuss   Present

1. What energy transformation powers your water wheel?

2. What happens when water is poured onto your water wheel from a greater height? Explain your results. With your classmates, discuss how the height of the water could affect the design of a dam and the reservoir behind it.

3. Use a table or chart to present the results you obtained when you changed the number, shape, or size of the flaps on your water wheel. Below your table or chart, explain which variable was being tested and which variables were kept the same.

4. Discuss with your group how your water wheel could be changed so it could produce electricity. Draw a picture of what this new water wheel could look like.

5. How does electricity get from hydro-electric power plants to your community? How do you know?

6. Do you think your community would be a good place to generate electricity using water as the energy source? Why or why not?

7. Add information to your energy sources table from Lesson 6 on the advantages and disadvantages of hydro-electricity.

8 Other Renewable Energy Sources

Even on a cold winter day, sunlight coming through a window can warm an entire room. The energy from the sun is called solar energy. It's free for everyone all over the world. The challenge is to capture this energy in a way that is useful when we need it. Like water power, solar energy is one of the renewable energy sources that could be used to replace some non-renewable ones. Other renewable energy sources include wind, biomass, tides, and heat from inside Earth.

As you read about these energy sources, think about the advantages and disadvantages of these energy sources.

Solar Energy

People have been using solar energy for a long time. To make the best use of it, three main technologies have been developed. These are collectors, reflectors, and solar cells.

Solar collectors are devices that collect heat from the sun. A solar collector can be as simple as a window that lets heat from the sun enter a home. This is called a **passive solar collector** because it has no moving parts. Other types of solar collectors contain water in tubes that are heated by the sun.

These solar collectors are usually located on the roof of a building. The hot water in the tubes is then pumped to other parts of the building where it can be used for washing or heating. These are called **active solar collectors** because the heated water is moved by using pumps.

This building uses a Trombe wall behind each glass panel. Trombe walls are made of thick concrete which absorbs heat from the sun and releases it into the interior of the building. The main draw-back to using solar collectors like a Trombe wall for heating is that the sun's energy may not be there when you need it most. At night or on very cloudy days, the sun cannot provide heat directly.

Solar reflectors focus the sun's energy onto one spot by using mirrors or lenses. That spot becomes so hot that if water is placed there, it changes to steam. Large solar reflectors can make enough steam to use in a generator to produce electricity. Small solar reflectors can be used to cook food.

Solar cells transform light energy into electrical energy. Any light energy will work with a solar cell—it doesn't have to be the sun's light. But large solar cells are too expensive to use where large amounts of electricity are needed. They are mainly used in places far from power lines and on space satellites.

Wind Energy

Wind energy is the energy of moving air. The sun heats Earth's surface unevenly. In warm spots, heated air rises. Cooler air then moves in to replace it. This moving air is wind.

Wind energy can be captured with sails or windmills. People have been using sails for over 5000 years to move boats on water. Windmills have been used for nearly 2000 years to pump water and grind grain. The wind turns the blades of a windmill, which then turn an attached shaft. The turning shaft can then power a water pump or an electricity generator.

In the next activity, you will investigate how a windmill moves in the wind.

These windmills are designed to capture the energy of the wind. They are connected to a generator for producing electrical energy. What problems do you think this technology has?

Materials for each student:

construction paper	scissors
ruler	pins
pencil with an eraser	

Procedure

1 Cut a 15-cm square out of construction paper.

2 Draw diagonals connecting the opposite corners of the square.

3 Cut along the diagonals to 1 cm from the centre.

4 Fold four alternating tips into the centre. Pin the four tips to the centre with a pin.

5 Pin the device to the eraser of the pencil.

6 Hold the opposite end of the pencil and blow on the blades of the windmill. What happens?

7 What do you think will happen if you blow on your windmill from behind or from the sides? Test your predictions.

Biomass Energy

You have probably warmed yourself by a pile of **biomass** at some time. Wood becomes biomass when it is chopped up for use in a fireplace, stove, or furnace. Biomass energy comes from fuels made from plant and animal waste. The most common kinds of biomass are wood, animal manure, and crop waste. These waste materials can be burned like fossil fuels for heat, or to produce electricity. They can also be processed to produce alcohol or methane, two chemicals that can be burned. Some gasoline companies process wheat to make alcohol, which they then add to their gasoline. This **gasohol** burns more cleanly than gasoline in car engines.

Are there any gasohol stations in your community?

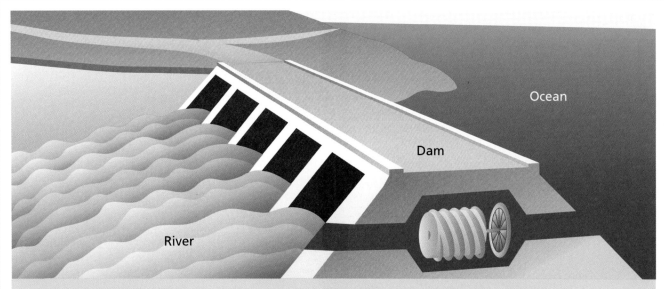

How does the water make the turbines spin at this tidal power station during high and low tides?

Tidal Energy

If you have ever been to the ocean, you might have noticed that the level of the water changes during the day. **Tides** are created by the pull of the moon and the sun on huge bodies of water. Scientists and engineers have designed power stations that use this tidal movement to produce electricity. The technology is similar to that used at hydro-electric power plants. The movement of the water is used to spin turbines connected to generators to make electricity. In Canada, the best place for a tidal power station is in the Bay of Fundy on the east coast. The highest tides in the world occur here. However, this technology is still new. It is very expensive and the effects on the environment are not yet well known.

Geothermal Energy

Geothermal energy is heat that comes from underground. It is usually in the form of hot water or steam. Geothermal energy can be used to heat buildings or turn turbines to create electricity. But geothermal energy is only useful when the energy source is close to Earth's surface.

Iceland is one country where geothermal energy is used successfully.

If Time Allows

What effect does the use of energy in your community have on the environment? How could you find out? Use the Internet and your local library to research one form of energy use in your community. Find out how it is affecting the environment where you live. Write 3 or 4 paragraphs about what you have found out and discuss it with your class.

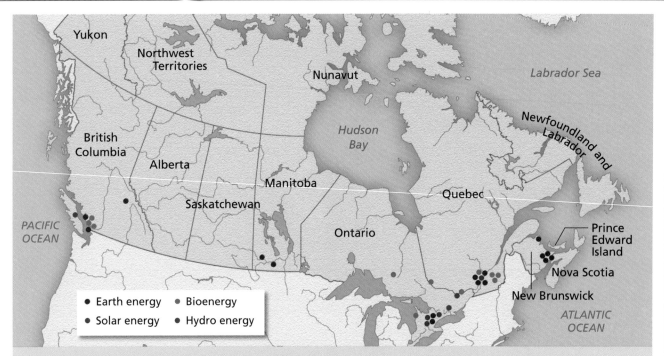

Canada is blessed with abundant renewable energy resources. This map shows the locations of the 34 renewable energy projects that form the Canadian Renewable Energy Network. These projects highlight some of the most current and innovative renewable energy technologies. (Bioenergy is biomass energy. Many Earth Energy projects use geothermal energy.)

This information is taken from the Atlas of Canada http://atlas.gc.ca. © 2003. Her Majesty the Queen in Right of Canada with permission of Natural Resources Canada.

Communicate

Write   Discuss

1. How do you think a solar reflector could be used to cook food? Draw a way that you could cook food, such as a hot dog or a marshmallow, using a solar reflector.

2. Why do you think companies that make calculators decide to use solar cells for them?

3. Discuss with your class some of the advantages and disadvantages of using solar power for heating homes, schools, and businesses. Add some of this information to your energy sources table from Lesson 6.

4. a. What happens when you blow lightly on your windmill? What happens when you blow hard?

   b. What happens when you blow on your windmill from different directions?

c. Discuss with a partner what wind conditions windmills need.

d. Should the windmill face the wind or have its face away from the wind? Explain your answer.

5. Why do you think wind power companies use many smaller windmills instead of one huge one?

6. Discuss with your classmates what effects using biomass energy could have on the environment.

7. Could a tidal power plant be built in the Great Lakes? Why or why not?

Build On What You Know

Are any of these renewable energy sources used in your community now? If so, write where and how they are used. Could more of these sources be used in your community? Explain where and how. Keep this information in your Energy File.

9 Technology and Energy Use

The 1998 ice storm in eastern Ontario and Quebec left thousands of people without electricity for weeks.

Get Started

If you like to watch television, imagine what your life would be like without it. Imagine what your life would be like without cars and trucks. How would you get to far-away places? How would you visit family and friends in other communities? Now imagine a cold, dark winter morning on a school day. You have to get out of bed in an unheated room. You have no electricity, so you can't just reach up and turn on a light. What would it be like not to have any hot water to wash in? You would experience life like this after a severe winter storm that brings down power lines, or if we run out of natural resources to produce electricity.

Work On It

You have learned in this unit how energy use has increased greatly in the past 250 years. More technology in the form of machines and other devices has made our lives easier. But it has also increased our energy use, especially of non-renewable energy sources. Today, scientists and engineers are designing machines and devices that can do work using as little energy as possible. Technology is also changing the way we use energy.

Have you ever sat next to a lamp and felt the warmth from the bulb? Ordinary light bulbs give us a very useful form of energy—light energy—but they aren't very good at producing it. Remember that transformation of electrical energy into light energy makes light bulbs work. The problem is that much of the electrical energy isn't transformed into light energy at all. Most of it transforms into heat! Only about 5% of the energy from an ordinary light bulb is useful as light energy. The other 95% is wasted as heat.

Fluorescent light bulbs are a different kind of light bulb. You see them in the ceiling at school and in shopping malls. You can buy fluorescent bulbs to use at home. Fluorescent bulbs are more efficient than ordinary light bulbs. They are designed so that about 20% of the electrical energy that goes into a fluorescent light bulb is transformed into light energy. Fluorescent bulbs cost more than ordinary light bulbs. However, they last longer and produce more light from less energy, so they are more economical than ordinary light bulbs.

Now read about some of the other ways technology is helping us use energy more effectively and economically. Make a list of the types of technology you and your family use now. Make another list of the ones you think you might use in the future.

In the past, cars were larger and made of heavy materials. They had big engines that used a lot of gasoline.

In the 1970s, car makers started designing smaller cars made of lighter materials. Today, most cars have smaller engines that burn fuel efficiently. These changes to cars and trucks mean that we use much less fuel now than we did with older vehicle designs.

5% useful energy

20% useful energy

Houses built in Canada today all have insulation in the walls and ceilings. Insulation is a special material used to keep heat in. Without insulation, a house in winter will cool down quickly, and the furnace must add more heat. A smaller furnace that uses less fuel can be used to heat an insulated house, saving people energy and money.

Computerized control systems, timers, and other control devices help us manage our use of energy better. Your furnace can be programmed to be on when you and your family are at home, and be off when everyone is out during the day at work or at school. If the furnace isn't on, it isn't using fuel.

Special labelling of products tell us which products are using the latest energy-saving technologies.

New home furnaces can transform more chemical energy to heat from the same amount of fuel than older furnaces can.

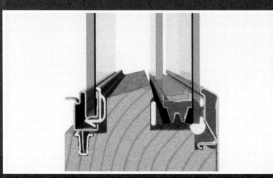

Older houses usually have windows with only one layer of glass. Newer houses have windows that have two or three layers of glass. These windows are better at keeping heat inside.

Special outdoor lights like the one in the picture have a sensing device that turns them on only when there is someone or something close by. The rest of the time they are off, saving energy.

1. Can you think of a technology such as a machine or a device your family has that uses a lot of energy? What can you and your family do to use less energy with this device?

2. Do you think your family will use any of the technologies described in this section in the future? Which ones? Why these?

3. Make a list of ten things you can do to consume less energy from electricity, oil (gasoline), and natural gas. Think of your home, your method of transportation, what you do on vacation, etc.

4. The car in the picture runs on electricity. Its top speed is about 50 km/h. For energy, it has a battery that has to be plugged in every night. This battery stores electricity so the car can run during the day.

   a. Do you think many people would buy a car like this? Why or why not?

   b. This car is only experimental. What improvements do you think the car maker needs to add so more people will be interested in this technology?

Build On What You Know

Draw a floor plan of your home like the one in this diagram. Label the rooms. For each room, show where you would add energy-saving technology if you could. For example, in the kitchen, you might want to put in a new fridge and stove that don't waste as much energy as the old ones. In the bathroom, you might want to put in a shower head that lessens the flow of hot water. Keep your floor plan in your Energy File.

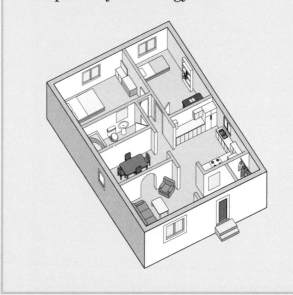

City-Coupé

10 Conserving Energy

Get Started

Conserving energy means using energy wisely so we use less. Some experts estimate that the world will run out of fossil fuels within the next 50 years. Other energy sources cannot easily replace fossil fuels. Hydro-electricity is clean, but building dams often floods large areas of land, displacing people and wildlife. Our current use of nuclear energy still has safety concerns. Renewable sources like wind and solar energy can help, but they also have drawbacks. Most of them cannot be stored easily, so they are not available all the time. Some are too expensive when used to produce large amounts of energy. So, until scientists and engineers can discover new energy sources or ways to better use the ones we have, we need to use energy more wisely.

The limited supply of fossil fuels is one reason to conserve energy. Another good reason is to protect the environment. Burning fossil fuels in cars or by industry pollutes the air we breathe. Now, many scientists believe that our use of fossil fuels is changing Earth's climate. Much of the sun's energy that reaches Earth is absorbed by Earth's surface. Some of this absorbed energy is released into the atmosphere as heat. Water vapour, carbon dioxide, and other gases in the atmosphere help to trap this heat, keeping it from going into space. This keeps Earth warm. The trapping of heat is called the **greenhouse effect**. Without this effect, Earth would be too cold for life to exist. Burning fossil fuels produces large amounts of carbon dioxide and other gases. Excessive amounts of these gases trap even more heat and cause temperatures around the world to rise. This is called **global warming**.

Warmer temperatures may sound like a good idea, but they can cause weather problems around the world. They could also cause the ice caps at the North and South Poles to melt. This extra water in the oceans would cause flooding in cities along coastal areas.

So what can we do to conserve energy? It is important to remember that large problems can be solved by people doing many little things. What are you and your friends willing to do? In the next activity, you get to tell the world about your best ideas for conserving energy.

Materials for each group:

pencil   paper

any other materials you may choose

Procedure

1 In a group, brainstorm ways that people can reduce the amount of energy they use.

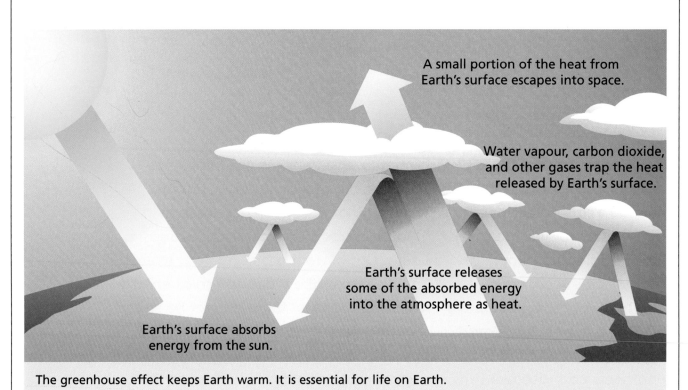

A small portion of the heat from Earth's surface escapes into space.

Water vapour, carbon dioxide, and other gases trap the heat released by Earth's surface.

Earth's surface releases some of the absorbed energy into the atmosphere as heat.

Earth's surface absorbs energy from the sun.

The greenhouse effect keeps Earth warm. It is essential for life on Earth.

2 Make a list of what people can do. Here are some suggestions.

- Walk, bike, or take the bus to school instead of being driven in a car.
- Turn off lights when no one needs them.
- Take shorter showers.

3 Choose three energy-saving suggestions from your list and do further research on them. Look for information on conserving energy in books and pamphlets from governments, the Internet, environmental groups, and energy service companies like gas companies or your provincial power generation company.

4 Select the two best ideas as the subject of your energy-saving program. These ideas should be things that will save energy and that people will be willing to do. For example, not driving cars will save energy, but most people would not be willing to completely stop driving their cars.

5 Now you are ready to advertise your best ideas. Decide on a way to tell people what they could do to save energy. You could write and perform a play or song. You could make a commercial or documentary and tape it with a video camera. You could draw posters to be displayed around the school. Or, you could choose another way to send your message.

Communicate Write

1. Do you think conserving energy is important? Why or why not?

2. Write a letter to the editor of your local newspaper about conserving energy. Suggest ways that people in your community could save energy. Make sure that you offer suggestions for other ways to do the same task. For example, you could suggest that people not use their clothes dryer every time they do their laundry. Instead, they could hang their clothes on a clothes line on sunny days.

3. Explain the saying, "Small deeds done are better than great deeds planned." How does this relate to conserving energy?

4. Explain how each of the following will encourage people to conserve energy. Which do you think would work better? Why?
   a. Save the environment.
   b. Save money.

Build On What You Know

Look at your chart of home energy uses in your Energy File. Use this chart to create a list of ways your family could save energy at home. Hold a family meeting to discuss these ideas. Choose two ways that you all agree to try for a week. After a week, meet again and discuss how your plan is working. Add other suggestions as you try to conserve energy. How do these changes affect your life? Open your Energy File every few weeks and talk to your family about trying a new way to conserve energy.

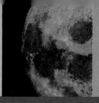

Designing for the Future

Get Started

In this unit, you have learned about the many ways that we use energy in our lives. You have also learned about the sources of energy that we use. Along the way, you learned that there is a limited supply of natural resources like coal, oil, natural gas, and uranium. There are also problems with their use. Some of the problems are environmental. Others are related to technology costs. But these problems will be solved by people like you, who think about the future. You and your friends can create solutions that haven't even been dreamed of today.

Look at the photographs on these pages. What examples do you see in these photos of ways that we can use energy better or reduce energy use?

Everyone can conserve energy—from individual students to big companies and governments. You have already suggested ways that you and your friends can change the way you use energy. Day-to-day activities like taking the bus instead of the car, and turning down the thermostat, all make a difference.

Another way to make a difference is in designing new energy-efficient buildings. In Canada, heating, lighting, and appliances in buildings are a big part of our energy use. Think of the difference you could make to your family's energy use by designing a new home that would conserve energy.

Work with a small group of your classmates to make a list of features you would include in an energy-efficient house. Think about these questions as you make your list.

- What would you do to make the house structure as energy efficient as possible? Think about the walls, windows, doors, roof, and basement.
- What could you do to save energy when you live in the house? Think about lights, appliances, the heating system, and hot water.
- What kinds of timers, sensing devices, or other controls could help you reduce energy use?
- What else could you do to reduce the amount of non-renewable energy sources you use?
- What other energy sources could you use?

Design Project

Now imagine that a family in your community wants to create a house of the future. They want your help in designing a house that will use energy wisely.

Materials for each group:

pencil   paper

various materials you need to build your model, such as Styrofoam, paper, cardboard, Plasticine

Procedure

1 In a group, use your list of house features to brainstorm ideas for the house you want to build. You could use the design of a house you have already seen, and improve on it. Or, you could design a house of your own. Discuss what materials you would use for a real house and record this information.

2 Draw several sketches of your house. Choose the best design.

3 When you have built your model house, you will present it to your classmates. You will explain how your house conserves energy and uses different sources of energy. Think about the following questions as you plan your model.

- What materials will you use for your model? These will be different from the materials you would use if you were building a real house.

- How will you show the energy coming in from different sources?

- How will you show energy-conserving appliances or control devices?

You may want to use different ways of presenting some of the information about your house, along with the model. You could use charts, drawings, posters, computer images, or other methods.

4 Build your model of the house of the future.

Communicate

Write Present

1. How many different energy sources does your home use? Explain.

2. How does your home conserve energy? Explain.

3. Does your home need to be built in a specific place? For example, does it need high winds, or sunny weather, etc.

4. Demonstrate your house to your classmates.

Review

Demonstrate What You Know

Get Started

Now it's time to show how much you have learned about energy and conserving energy. Read over what your tasks are, and talk to your teacher if you are unclear about what to do.

Work On It

1. Look at the community shown above. Make a list of the forms of energy that you see. Describe any energy transformations that you can identify.

2. Read your list of the forms of energy that you can see in the picture. Which are from non-renewable sources, and which are from renewable ones?

3. Suggest three ways that people in the picture could use less energy.

4. Now check your work. My work:

   ✓ lists different forms of energy in the picture

   ✓ describes some energy transformations

   ✓ lists sources of energy being used

   ✓ suggests three ways that people in the picture could use less energy.

Unit 3

Review

Communicate

Now it's time to think about how well you did. Use this chart to help you score your work. Four stars is the highest score for each.

1 Star	2 Stars	3 Stars	4 Stars
☆	☆☆	☆☆☆	☆☆☆☆

- **How much do you know about forms of energy? Look at your list of forms of energy. Does your work show you know**

A little about forms of energy	Some information about forms of energy	A lot of information about forms of energy	All about forms of energy?

- **Look at your descriptions of energy transformations. Does your work show you have**

A few of the skills to describe energy transformations	Some of the skills to describe energy transformations	**Most of the skills to describe energy transformations**	All of the skills to describe energy transformations?

- **Now look again at your descriptions. Will they be clear and precise to a reader?**

Not very clear or precise	Somewhat clear and precise	**Mostly clear and precise**	Very clear and precise

- **Look at your suggestions for ways people can conserve energy. How well do you think you understand how people could conserve energy?**

Not much understanding	Some understanding	**A good understanding**	A complete understanding

Write a short note explaining how well you think you did.

Explain Your Stuff

What did you learn about energy and conserving energy?

1. List ten forms of energy. Give a brief description of each form.

2. What is an energy transformation? Use a drawing to explain one example of an energy transformation.

3. Describe the energy transformations shown in the photos below. If there is more than one final form of energy, list all.

a. A log burning in a fireplace.

b. Someone hitting a drum.

c. An apple falling from a tree.

4. Name three energy transformations you rely on to survive.

5. List four ways that you use energy in your daily life. What is the energy source for each? Explain the effect that using these sources has on the environment.

6. Give an example of a non-renewable energy source. Explain its advantages and disadvantages.

7. Give an example of a renewable energy source. Explain its advantages and disadvantages.

8. Explain how technology can both increase and decrease energy use in our lives.

9. Give three examples of how you and the people in your community could conserve energy.

10. Which sources of energy will become more important in the future in your community? Give some reasons why.

How Did You Do?

1. List three things you didn't know about energy and conserving energy before this unit started.

2. What activities did you enjoy the most? Why? What activities did you like the least? Why?

3. Give yourself a pat on the back! What did you do well in this unit?

4. List any questions you still have about energy and conserving energy.

Now you know a lot of things about energy and conserving energy! Here are some of the things you've learned:

- Energy is useful because of what it does in our lives.

- There are many forms of energy: heat, light, sound, chemical, mechanical, electrical, elastic, magnetic, gravitational, and nuclear.

- Energy can be transformed from one form to another. Energy cannot be created or destroyed.

- During an energy transformation, not all the energy is transformed into a useful form of energy. An energy transformation is efficient if it transforms much of the input energy to useful energy.

- There are many sources of energy. Some sources of energy are renewable and others are non-renewable.

- Renewable energy sources are ones that can be replaced in a short time.

- Non-renewable energy sources are ones that cannot be replaced in a short time, or cannot ever be replaced.

- Technology has increased the number of energy devices we use every day, but it has also improved these devices so they use energy more efficiently.

- We can do many things to conserve energy and use it more wisely.

Glossary

acid rain rain that contains acids that can damage lakes, soil, and plants

acid snow snow that contains acids that can damage lakes, soil, and plants

active solar collector a device with moving parts that is used to absorb energy from the sun

biomass plant and animal waste, like wood or animal manure; can be burned for heat

chemical energy the stored energy in substances that can be released in chemical reactions

elastic energy the stored energy an object has when its shape is changed by stretching or compressing

electrical energy the energy we use to activate parts in our machines, such as televisions and computers

energy the ability to make things move and do work

energy transformation the changing of energy from one form to another

fossil fuel coal, oil, and natural gas; they are formed over millions of years from dead plants and animals under a lot of pressure and heat beneath Earth's surface

gasohol fuel made by mixing gasoline with alcohol

geothermal energy heat that comes from underground, usually in the form of hot water or steam

global warming the slow increase in temperature around the world due to the increase in the amount of carbon dioxide gas and other gases in the atmosphere

gravitational energy the stored energy something has because of its position above Earth's surface

greenhouse effect the trapping of heat from Earth's surface by water vapour, carbon dioxide, and other gases in the atmosphere

heat thermal energy; the type of energy in every object that gives it temperature; the more heat an object has, the warmer it feels; the less heat an object has, the cooler it feels

hydro-electric power plant an electricity-generating station that uses moving water as the energy source

hydro-electricity electricity produced by transforming the energy in moving water into electrical energy; hydro means water

kinetic energy the energy of moving objects

light energy the form of energy that allows us to see things

magnetic energy the energy stored in some magnet systems

mechanical energy the energy due to movement or position of an object

natural resource any material from nature that is used by humans

non-renewable energy source a source of energy that is hard to replace or cannot be replaced once it is used up, such as coal, oil, natural gas, and uranium

nuclear energy the energy stored deep inside matter

nuclear generating station an electricity-generating station that uses nuclear energy as the energy source

oil boom a floating device used by clean-up crews to contain an oil spill

passive solar collector a device with no moving parts that is used to absorb energy from the sun

potential energy stored energy

renewable energy source a source of energy that can be easily replaced, such as sunlight, water, and wind

Glossary

reservoir a human-made lake, usually created by building a dam on a river, flooding the land behind the dam

solar cells devices that transform light energy into electrical energy

solar reflectors mirrors or lenses that focus the sun's energy onto one spot

sound energy the energy produced when matter vibrates

source of energy a material that is used to produce energy we can use

tides the slow rise and fall of the water level at the shoreline of oceans or other large bodies of water; created by the pull of the moon and the sun on huge bodies of water

turbines huge, specially designed wheels used in power plants; steam or water spin turbines very quickly to produce electricity in generators

variables all the things that could affect what happens in an experiment

Acknowledgments

The publisher wishes to thank the following sources for photographs, illustrations, articles, and other materials used in this book. Care has been taken to determine and locate ownership of copyrighted material used in this text. We will gladly receive information enabling us to rectify any errors or omissions in credits.

Photography

p. 1 (centre) R. Watts/First Light, p. 1 (bottom) PhotoDisc, Inc., p. 5 Ray Boudreau, p. 6 Ray Boudreau, p. 7 Ivy Images, p. 8 (top left) Dave Starrett, p. 8 (top right) PhotoDisc, Inc., p. 8 (centre left) Bob Krist/CORBIS, p. 8 (centre right) Artbase Inc., p. 8 (bottom left) PhotoDisc, Inc., p. 8 (bottom right) Artbase Inc., p. 9 (from top to bottom) Dave Starrett, PhotoDisc, Inc., Artbase Inc., Dave Starrett, p. 10 Dave Starrett, p. 11 Ray Boudreau, p. 12 Ray Boudreau, p. 13 Ray Boudreau, p. 17 Corbis, p. 18 Corel Stock Photo Library, p. 19 (top) Benjamin Rondel/First Light, p. 19 (bottom) National Renewable Energy Laboratory/DOE/NREL–Pix #02562, p. 20 L. MacDougal/First Light, p. 23 Vince Streano/Tony Stone Images, p. 25 David Woodfall/Tony Stone Images, p. 27 Ed Simpson/Tony Stone Images, p. 28 (bottom) Thomas Kitchin/First Light, p. 29 Ray Boudreau, p. 31 Ivy Images, p. 32 (top) Ivy Images, p. 32 (bottom) National Renewable Energy Laboratory, p. 33 (top left) National Renewable Energy Laboratory/DOE/NREL–Pix #02320, p. 33 (top right) Laurence Dutton/Tony Stone Images, p. 33 (bottom) Alan Sirulnikoff/First Light, p. 34 (top) Ray Boudreau, p. 34 (bottom) Dick Hemingway: Photographs, p. 35 Jamey Stillings/Tony Stone Images, p. 37 Sean O'Neill/Ivy Images, p. 38 (top right) Trevor Wood/Tony Stone Images, p. 38 (bottom right) Trevor Bonderud/First Light, p. 38 (bottom left) Dave Starrett, p. 39 (top left) Dick Hemingway: Photographs, p. 39 (top right) Dick Hemingway: Photographs, p. 39 (centre left) Dick Hemingway: Photographs, p. 39 (centre right) Trent Metals Ltd., p. 39 (bottom right) Ivy Images, p. 39 (bottom left) SmartSash™ III from PELLA™/Kaycan Ltd., p. 40 CP Picture Archive, p. 44 (bottom) Ivy Images, p. 45 (top) Ivy Images, p. 45 (centre) National Renewable Energy Laboratory/DOE/NREL–Pix #04924, p. 45 (bottom) Dick Hemingway: Photographs, p. 49 (top) Michael Melford/Image Bank, p. 49 (centre) Thomas Del Brase/Tony Stone Images, p. 49 (bottom) Ivy Images

Illustration

Crowle Art Group: p. 36
Jun Park: p. 21, p. 22, p. 23 (bottom), p. 24, p. 28 (top), p. 30, p. 35 (top), p. 40 (top), p. 42
Dave Whamond: pp. 2–3, p. 4, p. 14, p. 16, p. 41, p. 47

Cover Photograph

Glen Allison/Tony Stone Images